IN THE
NATIONAL INTEREST

General Sir John Monash once exhorted a graduating class to 'equip yourself for life, not solely for your own benefit but for the benefit of the whole community'. At the university established in his name, we repeat this statement to our own graduating classes, to acknowledge how important it is that common or public good flows from education.

Universities spread and build on the knowledge they acquire through scholarship in many ways, well beyond the transmission of this learning through education. It is a necessary part of a university's role to debate its findings, not only with other researchers and scholars, but also with the broader community in which it resides.

Publishing for the benefit of society is an important part of a university's commitment to free intellectual inquiry. A university provides civil space for such inquiry by its scholars, as well as for investigations by public intellectuals and expert practitioners.

This series, In the National Interest, embodies Monash University's mission to extend knowledge and encourage informed debate about matters of great significance to Australia's future.

Professor Margaret Gardner AC
President and Vice-Chancellor,
Monash University

CAMPBELL WILSON
LIVING WITH AI

MONASH
UNIVERSITY
PUBLISHING

Living with AI

© Copyright 2023 Campbell Wilson

All rights reserved. Apart from any uses permitted by Australia's *Copyright Act 1968*, no part of this book may be reproduced by any process without prior written permission from the copyright owners. Inquiries should be directed to the publisher.

Monash University Publishing
Matheson Library Annexe
40 Exhibition Walk
Monash University
Clayton, Victoria 3800, Australia
https://publishing.monash.edu

Monash University Publishing brings to the world publications which advance the best traditions of humane and enlightened thought.

ISBN: 9781922979049 (paperback)
ISBN: 9781922979063 (ebook)

Series: In the National Interest
Editor: Greg Bain
Project manager & copyeditor: Paul Smitz
Designer: Peter Long
Typesetter: Cannon Typesetting
Proofreader: Gillian Armitage
Printed in Australia by Ligare Book Printers

A catalogue record for this book is available from the National Library of Australia.

The paper this book is printed on is in accordance with the standards of the Forest Stewardship Council®. The FSC® promotes environmentally responsible, socially beneficial and economically viable management of the world's forests.

LIVING WITH AI

AI—artificial intelligence—is hard to avoid because it's everywhere. It's simultaneously the subject of massive research and commercial investment, government anxiety over its possible regulation, breathless marketing hype and plenty of excitement mixed with some consternation in the community at large.

It might seem to be a relatively new addition to the world, but it's not really. AI has been around, at least as a research field, for well over fifty years. But in the last decade, what was a slow increase in prominence has accelerated, as AI has shown itself to be an enormously potent technology. It has well and truly sprung out of the research shadows and straight into public discourse. One recent example is OpenAI's ChatGPT chatbot (and associated GPT-4 language model), which captured the world's imagination in early 2023.[1] Many were astounded by ChatGPT's uncanny ability to emulate human language and engage in spookily coherent dialogue with real people. But these systems are just the tip of the AI iceberg.

In business, money is racing out the door in pursuit of AI development. Stanford University reported that, in 2021, global private investment in AI topped US$93 billion.[2] McKinsey, in a 2022 review of AI adoption, reported that half of the businesses surveyed had deployed AI in one of their functions—topping the list of these AI technologies were robotic process automation, computer vision and language understanding.[3] And a recent PwC report estimated that, by 2030, AI will be contributing well over US$15 trillion to the global economy.[4]

At the individual level, there's an understandable clamour of interest in the AI algorithms that are increasingly influencing our lives. Maybe you won't interact with an 'intelligent chatbot' on the day you read this, but it's likely you will engage with an AI system in some way today. That might be through using a search engine. Or perhaps you'll have a useful voice interaction with a non-human AI device sitting on a shelf. In many homes, these so-called smart digital assistants, such as Google Home and Amazon Alexa, eavesdrop on all conversations, listening for trigger words that prompt them to spring into action, connecting with algorithms on distant servers to answer any and all manner of questions. Maybe you'll be observed by AI-run cameras at a supermarket checkout, having bought products that were probably positioned in the store relative to other products based on what a smart algorithm predicted would best increase sales.

There are many other ways in which we interact with AI. It curates our entertainment, scrutinising our listening and watching habits so that it can suggest content it thinks we will love—along the way feeding us advertising based on AI assessments of where we most likely want to spend our money. Some houses are patrolled by robotic vacuum cleaners that use cameras to autonomously map rooms and avoid pesky obstacles in their quest to eliminate dust in the most effective manner possible. Of course, the most potent vector through which AI invades our lives is that very powerful computer called a mobile phone which we happily carry around with us. Phones are chock-full of AI that corrects the spelling of our texts, recognises our faces and those of others, helps us find the quickest way around town, even enhances our cinematography skills as we capture life's everyday moments.

Plenty of people drive cars full of AI-assisted driving aids—some, cars with AI powerful enough to take over all of the driving—along roads monitored by AI-enabled traffic-management cameras, to eventually stop in car parks whose gatekeepers are cameras that silently perform automated number-plate recognition. In offices, we may ride AI-powered elevators to then sit at desks where we process email communications filtered by AI. Factories are increasingly becoming stacked with robots, and automation more broadly is transforming workplaces and the nature of industry. Medical laboratories make use of AI in their research activities, including the design of new drugs. Financial institutions use AI to detect fraud at scale, while algorithmic trading is beginning to dominate stock markets. It's hard to argue with the assertion that, considering its ubiquity, AI is a pretty hot topic.

There is a panoply of issues to dig into with respect to AI. First, can we easily define it? And how does it work? Naturally, there's a lot of technology at play in AI systems, and that could involve a very deep dive. To begin with, I'll outline some basic principles concerning how AI functions. But, as with all technology, how it works needs to be contextualised with how (and why) it is used. When it comes to working out how we choose to live with AI, the latter is perhaps the most important question. That's why, as well as touching on the technical details, I'll also explore issues of consent, ethics, weaponisation, explainability and transparency.

THE INTELLIGENT MACHINE

What is AI really? From a technological point of view, it is a concept now having its moment in the sun. The very idea of 'intelligent machines' has long fascinated scientists, philosophers and writers, but it wasn't until the middle of last century that tools with the potential to realise such machines arrived, in the form of the first digital computers.[5] Since then, with a few bumps along the way, steady progress has been made in the pursuit of what we now call AI.

What is commonly understood about computers is that they do their work by processing input data, following instructions encoded in their software, and consequently produce some kind of output. Reflecting this, early attempts to achieve what were passably 'smart' computing systems involved encoding rules about the world, specifically those that could be programmed in software. The idea was that the computer could make decisions by applying these rules, which were meticulously crafted by programmers, to a variety of inputs. The limitation of what was labelled the *expert system* was that compiling a finite set of rules to adequately describe the real world, and have that evolve over time, was not just difficult but ultimately—in a general sense—intractable.

The hope was that, in narrow-enough domains, this at least would be good enough for some forms of basic automation. And these systems were indeed useful in fundamental ways. But they could not be relied on to provide more generalised and capable decision-making support.

We've come a long way since those early expert systems, and it has been quite a journey for computer science. As with many longstanding scientific endeavours, the path from that dawn of digital computing through to today's AI is decorated with milestones, many of which provided seismic shifts in progress. But it's also flanked by a fair number of dead-end efforts that for a time seemed promising. I'm not setting out to tell the full story of how AI got to where it is today. If you're interested in that tale, there are many books and articles out there which cover the history of AI in depth—and it's truly a fascinating story. It's simply worth acknowledging that while it might seem like a recent advance, today's AI has actually been a long time coming. And its development continues apace.

You'd think it would make sense to open a discussion of AI by just defining it, but it's not that straightforward. The term *artificial intelligence* originally was used by scientists who were interested in exploring the limits of machines in simulating intelligent human behaviour. They were fairly clear about the sorts of human capacities they wanted to feign and framed artificial intelligence around these goals. But generalising beyond a finite list of things to simulate—with some being very complex in and of themselves, such as, for example, language understanding—is where it all gets messy. The notion of characterising intelligence in a computational sense is particularly fraught. The debate as to whether a computer program can ever really be intelligent at all is not going away anytime soon.

The brilliant mathematician and oft-denoted father of computer science Alan Turing posed the question 'Can machines think?' in a seminal paper published in 1950.[6] He opined that, in this context, attempting to formally define the word 'think' was ultimately pointless, which echoes the dilemma in defining 'intelligence' when discussing AI today. This has been exacerbated by the coopting of the phrase 'artificial intelligence' in all sorts of hype-driven ways, and some (occasionally outlandish) post-hoc claims about the human-level features of the technology. To make things worse, AI also has been retrospectively applied as a label to algorithms that were originally described otherwise. After all, it's a nice addition to a marketing blurb to say a product is 'intelligent' compared with drier—and perhaps harder to spruik—descriptions such as 'data analysis tool' or 'statistics software'.

FROM IMITATION TO DEEP LEARNING

The difficulties of definition notwithstanding, let's move beyond an intuitive feeling of what AI is and settle on an understanding of some of its basic characteristics. The key element common to most descriptions of the nature of AI is that the technology 'simulates', 'imitates' or 'acts like' intelligent human beings; however, it is also generally accepted that AI performs tasks that would require relatively *complex* decision-making or reasoning. For example, an intelligent human being can perform the addition of two numbers, but a computer performing the same task and therefore simulating the behaviour of that same intelligent human would not normally be considered an intelligent system as such.[7] Indeed, many would say that for AI to deserve its moniker, it should perform tasks that 'traditionally' could not be performed by computers, only by humans; or even that AI should inherently surprise or shock human beings with its degree of so-called 'intelligence'.

When it comes to how AI is put together, things also are a little complicated. There's more than one way to skin the metaphorical AI cat. Today's AI systems can be built using one or more of many available tools and techniques. So, be prepared—if you ask a computer scientist how AI works, you're quite likely to get a response (and a facial expression) similar to that from a mechanical engineer when asked how transportation works. That is, AI is a pretty general concept and many different sub-domains lie under the AI umbrella.

The most prominent technology enabling AI systems to perform their magic is known as *machine learning*. Computers are made up of hardware, or the physical components of the machine, and software, or the instructions that tell the hardware what to do. In a machine learning system, the instructions in the software don't just tell the computer to follow steps that lead directly to the solution of a problem. Rather, they tell the computer to *learn* how to solve certain problems through the analysis of input data. Further, in *supervised machine learning*, in addition to input data, the computer's learning is steered by it being told something about what it *should* be producing as output. During this training phase, it is essentially expected to learn functions that minimise the difference between the input and the desired output. Once these functions are learned, they can be applied to input data the machine has never been exposed to before, in the hope that this new data will be correctly mapped to the desirable output.

This sort of thing might sound familiar: statistical data analysis has long been concerned with similar tasks. For example, upon analysis of a dataset of the sale prices of houses in a city during a particular time window, there are well-established techniques for building a function that will predict the sale price of a house new to the market with reasonable accuracy. AI systems, however, often deal with functions that are much more difficult to compute than more basic statistical systems—they excel in learning about very complex relationships between input data and the desired output.

Consider a feature built into phones and other devices that can automatically detect classes of objects in photos. For example, typing the word 'car' into the search bar of a mobile photo application ideally results in the rapid display of, yes, photos of cars. In order for this to happen, the software in the phone must show off its ability to take input in the form of an English word and map that to the relevant images. This is a machine learning system at work. And it's all based on numbers—lots of them. Behind the scenes, a set of functions is being used to map the numbers representing the images to those numbers representing all the classes of objects the phone is able to find (with 'car' being one of these).[8] When you buy your phone, it comes with pre-trained machine learning models built in that have already *learnt* these functions, telling it what cars and all these other object classes are—or, more precisely, what combination of visual features are most likely to represent the object class.

The state-of-the-art AI technology that enables this kind of computation is a supercharged form of machine learning known as *deep learning*. Most deep learning systems are a relatively recent evolution of systems based on artificial neural networks, inspired by the architecture of the human brain. The fundamental bases of neural networks were first postulated well over fifty years ago, and research into how they can be most effectively and efficiently scaled to attack problems of classifying data and making various predictions has occupied many computer scientists over a great number of years. Neural network mechanisms have fallen in and out of favour at various points of AI's history, but they are well and truly back in vogue now in their deep learning form.

Deep learning is just one of multiple tools used for building AI. But it's the engine that, in tandem with rapid growth in fast and scalable computing power, has driven much of the technology's recent achievements. It's how that photo application on your phone can tell you exactly which images contain cars, trees, furniture, sunsets and so on. Deep learning also has enabled more broadly applicable *computer vision*, which is scarily accurate and efficient. This sort of AI helps autonomous vehicles navigate their way around the world in real time.

What goes on inside deep learning artificial neural networks? To get technical for a minute, you can think of them as combinations of many simple, individual calculating units that take a number as input, perform some basic maths with that number, and produce a number as output. Crucially, within the network, there are a lot of connections between these calculating units. The strength of each of these connections is indicated by a number called a *weight*, and the weights in a network form the lion's share of a collection of numbers called *parameters*, which basically encode the network's power. A high level of connectivity in a network, coupled with some ingenious mathematical data processing, allows it to adjust its own parameters during training. In turn, this adjustment process allows the network to learn very complex functions. In our photo app example, it is those learnt functions that ensure an image fed into the network gets classified correctly based on its content. In a computer vision deep learning network, hundreds of millions—or in some cases hundreds of billions—of individual parameters may be computed during training.

We're skipping over a lot of the detail here, but suffice to say that the ways in which deep learning networks are organised and trained, as well as the intricacies of other computational AI techniques, make up a hugely active domain of research. It's not clear how far deep learning approaches will take us as AI advances, but they certainly have enabled some revolutionary progress so far.

THE CREATIVITY OF AI

As well as dealing with computer vision scenarios, AI systems also have made huge inroads into recognising and even generating that most human characteristic: language. *Natural language processing systems* have been shown to be very proficient in what is, like computer vision, a wickedly difficult problem space. One of the many challenges in approaching language from a computational point of view is that not only is the order of words important in conveying the overall meaning of text, there also are both short- and long-range contexts at play. That is, what has been written at a particular point in a text relates not only to nearby words but also to those further afield, and, to various degrees, to the overall narrative. AI has to remember those relationships as it is 'reading' and building its internal representation of the text in question. Recent advances in deep learning neural network architectures specifically have been aimed at processing input data such as text that have an inherent sequence and attempting to capture and represent this variable-range context. This has enabled very accurate machine translation from one language into another, more useful search engines, and a multitude of tools that can suggest how text might be redrafted or the grammar improved. Coupled with speech-to-text translation and information-retrieval technology, these kinds of systems help power an increasing number of those smart digital assistants that sit in many homes, answering questions from their owners and acting as a kind of computerised concierge.

But AI is not just being employed to analyse images, text and speech, or perform helpful tasks in response to this analysis. Increasingly it is being used to *create* new material—well, at least to produce material in a way that *seems* creative. The maxim that there is nothing new under the sun seems particularly well suited to the algorithms underlying the systems that have become known as *generative AI*. That is, while tools have been developed that seemingly have a remarkable aptitude for constructing images, text and music that have never been seen before, most of them are trained to do this by ingesting and mathematically analysing enormous amounts of data generated (as of now) mostly by humans. Those multibillion-parameter large language models based on deep learning such as ChatGPT, which are now the target of much discussion, are adept at writing text in response to human prompts. Other types of generative AI systems don't produce text, but rather ultra-realistic synthetic 'photographs' or plausibly artistic imagery that, while purely the output of a computer, look to be the product of a highly skilled human photographer or painter.

On the face of it, these AI systems can startle with their prowess. For example, ChatGPT produced the following text in response to my prompt asking it to rewrite the previous paragraph for a primary school readership:

AI is not just used for looking at pictures, reading words and listening to people talk. It's also used for making things! But it's not like how you and I make things. AI makes things using something called 'generative AI'. This means it can make new pictures, words and music that nobody has ever seen before. But, it has to learn how to do this by looking at a lot of information made by people. Now, there are computers that can even write words just by being asked to by a person.

While many question how 'intelligent' are the AI algorithms behind these systems, these arguments, while academically interesting, increasingly seem marginal in the current flurry of AI excitement. Yes, more rudimentary AI algorithms are based on statistical approaches to the analysis of data that are not particularly novel. We are now in an era where previously well-known approaches are being automated, augmented and applied in the form of what is described as AI at a scale never before seen. But, in addition to this relabelling of older techniques as AI, the next generation of algorithms such as deep learning are propelling smarter and smarter systems—such as ChatGPT and its siblings.

One of the drawbacks of labelling AI models as intelligent is that it encourages the anthropomorphising of the computer systems. The overuse of such descriptions can give incorrect impressions of a lack of human agency with respect to development of the technology. But this aside, we probably must—however grudgingly—accept the AI label.

THE BEST OR THE WORST THING

The question that naturally follows on from an analysis of the present state of AI is: where are we heading? Here, things quickly become philosophical. There is much debate as to if (or when, depending on who you ask) we will reach an age of artificial *general* intelligence (AGI), beyond the current era of so-called artificial *narrow* intelligence (ANI). In this context, 'narrow' refers to the fact that our current AI systems are very good at performing highly specific tasks, but they soon fall over when it comes to learning to generalise beyond those tasks. For example, a facial recognition AI and a natural language processing AI are trained and engineered for those tasks only and would not easily be able to perform functions outside of these domains. Human beings are capable of an intelligence much more powerful than that exhibited by ANI, across multiple domains of input. We make complex decisions very quickly based on all sorts of experiences as we continually learn from our environment, with sensory input mixing with various emotional and instinctive responses. Our brains are always constructing new connections and encoding new patterns as we build our mental models of the world. Furthermore, we naturally operate within communities, with our decision-making and actions shaped by internal and external social and moral frameworks. So is it possible that this could all be emulated computationally in the form of an AGI, or is this a hopelessly reductionist pipedream? Whether or not we are capable of engineering such an outcome is well and truly an open question.

Let's imagine an AGI eventually will be created. It would be a radically different beast compared with today's algorithms and systems. How we might interact with computers capable of human-level, general-purpose reasoning is truly the stuff of science fiction, as is the question of how such an AI would view human beings. Some even argue that, should an AGI be created, it may learn to improve itself in such a way that an artificial *super-intelligence* may result. Such an outcome could really get in the way of our abiding ambition as human beings to maintain the upper hand with respect to technology. An apocalyptic scenario would see us considered purely superfluous by such mega AI agents—we may well be out of the picture at that point, so to speak. The late theoretical physicist Stephen Hawking described the ultimate realisation of highly competent AI as 'either the best, or the worst thing, ever to happen to humanity'.[9] Some ask the question: could we, by pursuing this supercharged form of AI, be engineering our own replacement?

When we take a good look at today's AI systems, talk of the replacement of humanity might seem a laughably remote concept. However, some AIs are capable of very clever things. It's also useful to remember that the pace of recent advancements in AI have surprised many, including some of those researching in the field. Many of the discussions around the limitations of AI progression come down to rationalist versus empiricist arguments over the nature of cognition, and the thought experiments around the evolution of AGI will certainly continue. In the meantime, AI (or at least ANI) is well and truly impacting us in many ways. We need to think about how we are going to live with it, and what role we want it to play in our future.

FEVER PITCH: THE AI HYPE MACHINE

New machine learning algorithms and other forms of AI are being created, tested and deployed at an enormous rate, for all sorts of applications. And it's true that this is enabling beneficial transformation across many industries. For example, farming and agriculture are already benefiting from AI playing an increasingly bigger role in the vibrant 'AgTech' sector. Similarly, transportation, logistics, health care and education are all being positively impacted by AI in its various forms. There are use cases across all forms of endeavour. AI is rapidly maturing, and it will continue to enable functional automation and disrupt previous ways of working. Yes, many human jobs will ultimately be replaced. Undoubtedly, though, there will be a labour market shift to working alongside AI systems, creating new types of employment.

But AI marketing machines go way beyond just laying out the facts regarding how AI is helping us. Tech companies large and small are spruiking AI with all they've got. This, of course, is predictable given the vested commercial interests. Examples of AI hype abound. Tesla CEO Elon Musk drew criticism for over-egging AI when he unveiled the company's Optimus robot in 2021 and claimed it would eventually be able to perform any task that humans don't want to do.[10] That's a pretty big call. And in 2023, Microsoft breathlessly launched an AI chatbot service integrated with its search engine

Bing, only to quickly curtail its use and perform further testing after some especially problematic responses to users. Funnily enough, this has echoes of an earlier Microsoft chatbot called Tay that was based on a different type of AI model. Released in 2016, Tay was designed to operate on Twitter, learning from and interacting with social media users via tweets. Microsoft, in encouraging users to interact with Tay, marketed it as an 'AI with zero chill'.[11] Bad idea. Twitter doesn't enjoy a reputation for being the most friendly and respectful place, and it wasn't long before Tay was baited by some users into becoming hugely offensive, which led to it being withdrawn by Microsoft. In a sense, it had done its job—it learned from its users and tweeted in the way that many people do. But the rapid emergence of a racist and sexist AI could have been predicted. Rushing AI out the door to illustrate technical prowess was a case of hype before responsibility.

AI hype also happens at less-spectacular levels. In 2019, an oft-quoted Gartner report predicted that the success rate for many types of corporate AI projects was a dramatically low 15 per cent.[12]

It has been further reported that this figure has not changed much recently. One reason for this, among other things, is a clear tendency to overpromise and underdeliver with respect to the capabilities of AI. This has led to greater interest from regulators. In February 2023, in a blog post titled 'Keep Your AI Claims in Check', the US Federal Trade Commission cautioned advertisers not to exaggerate the proficiencies of AI systems nor claim something as being AI when it's not.[13]

On the sidelines of the commercial hype machines—and sometimes within them—a more technical battle is playing out among researchers. Scientific debate is nothing new; indeed, it is a fundamental necessity. But this one is particularly vociferous, with ferocious claims and counterclaims concerning AI's abilities and potential. A recent flare-up related to the large language models underlying tools like ChatGPT. Many computer scientists have warned of the risks of their widespread use, particularly as they could be inappropriately relied on or trusted by their users. This is because the models are so demonstrably proficient at generating text that looks as though it might have been written by humans. Others have gone further than this, claiming this kind of AI is actually capable of 'understanding', or in some cases demonstrates 'sentience'. It was big news in 2022 when former Google engineer Blake Lemoine publicly stated that his interactions with the company's Lamda AI language model showed it was demonstrating consciousness—at least equivalent to that of a small child. This sparked furious disagreement between those on both sides of the 'AI is close to being sentient' fence.

Some involved in AI research and development are even flagging the advent of artificial general intelligence much more explicitly. In February 2023, OpenAI CEO Sam Altman wrote in a blog post that should AGI be achieved, it would be a 'force multiplier' for human ingenuity and its development should not be curtailed. However, he also wrote that OpenAI believes that the 'future of humanity should be determined by humanity'.[14] It's great to know that this particular AI research centre is not a fan of the human race being governed by machines that pose existential threats. The rest of us surely echo their thoughts on that one.

More to the point, in some ways this is all a distraction from the big issues around AI at present, given the changes it will drive in the near future simply in its current form. So let's explore some of these issues, beginning with one of the most pressing—that of data and consent for its use.

TRAINING AI: WHERE DOES THE DATA COME FROM?

Not all AI systems use machine learning or deep learning, but those that do usually need to be trained. An AI can't learn without material to learn from. So, crucial to the capacity of AI systems to produce useful output is their dependency on what are often huge volumes of training data. In particular, in order for current deep learning networks to perform well, they need to be able to *generalise*. Here, I don't mean generalise in the sense of knowing everything it is possible to know about the world, but rather to generalise about data in its domain of application. We don't want the AI to merely be really good at knowing what it saw during its training phase; we also want it to be very good at dealing with data it *wasn't exposed to* during training. It turns out that, even if it works well during the training phase, tuning the large number of parameters in complex neural networks (remember, this could be in the hundreds of billions) so that they successfully generalise, may not work so well if you don't have enough data. It is said that, in this undesirable case, these networks are *overfitted* to the training data. And if that happens, we have an AI that's pretty much useless to us in the real world.

One of the ways of overcoming this problem is to increase the amount of training data—or, as computer scientists would say, get a bigger training set. There are other reasons for having a large training set, such as it helps provide a more comprehensive and hopefully representative picture of the environment. Of course, the size of this dataset is not the only factor at play here—large amounts of data skewed in some way is not a desirable scenario. But assuming we are able to deal with issues of representation, the question then is how much data does the AI really need, in order to get it to generalise well and be exposed to a good cross-section of its input domain. This is a question that AI researchers and developers grapple with all the time. There are plenty of 'rules of thumb' that have been developed for particular applications, but generally, the more complex the AI (for example, the larger and more connected the neural network), the more training data are required.[15]

Let's talk concrete numbers. ChatGPT was trained on a corpus of text in the order of tens of billions of words[16]—naturally, I discovered this by asking it. Google's comparable Lamda language model was trained on a corpus of 1.56 trillion words, similar to Meta AI's LLAMA language model. Although this is only a fraction of the number of words that exist in the world— Wikipedia's English word count alone was around 4.2 billion as of February 2023[17]—it is a seriously large amount of data. And it's not just text that AI is consuming in large quantities. Looking beyond AI language models, there are computer vision and image processing AI models similarly trained on massive amounts of images, in the order of tens to hundreds of millions of them. Stable Diffusion, a deep learning generative AI model that generates images based on text prompts, was trained on more than two billion pairs of images and text descriptions.[18] Other AI applications can get away with much less data than this. It all depends on the task the AI is asked to perform. The particularly powerful deep learning models tend to be the most data-hungry.

Now we come to a key question: where does all the data used to train AI models actually come from? Well, fortunately for AI developers, humans for a while now have been generating, storing and publishing data online in ever-escalating amounts. Estimates vary but active internet users are expected to number well over five billion by the close of 2023[19]—that's two thirds of the world's population. And there will be something in the order of 200 million active websites.[20] Not only are we all acting more and more like online digital information hoarders, but widespread adoption of social media has seen us sharing, duplicating and transforming this data at massive scale. This is gold to AI developers, who, if they can access it, will grab this data with enthusiasm to train their models—as

I explained earlier, more data often means better performance of the algorithm. Better yet, plenty of this data is publicly accessible, with no accounts or passwords required, and easily downloaded. On large social platforms, an enormous amount of data can be harvested very quickly. Often, the platforms even provide tools to AI developers allowing them do this harvesting more easily; that is, as long as they meet the service terms—data, after all, is very big business.

But it's not just raw data that AI needs. The data need to be annotated, or *labelled*. In training AI to recognise objects in an image, developers require the images to have labels indicating what objects they contain. We'll come back to this subject, because the way in which this labelling is undertaken sometimes presents thorny ethical challenges.

So, the open nature of the internet coupled with its voluminous data holdings provide a rich hunting ground for hungry AI. And it's here that one of the big dilemmas posed by AI rears its head. Just because data exists on the web, should anyone who happens to have the required amount of computational resources be able to use it to train and deploy AI systems, for any application they like?

THE DILEMMA OF CONSENT

In 2019, my team at Monash University, along with the Australian Federal Police (AFP), launched the AiLECS research laboratory. Yes, it's a weird thing to pronounce—we say it like 'Alex'—but the acronym describes the purpose of the collaboration: AI for law enforcement and community safety. A foundation project of the lab is research and development aimed at having AI, mostly computer vision via deep learning, identify illegal imagery. Specifically, we are developing algorithms to locate and triage some of the worst images that police have to deal with—those of the sexual exploitation of children. Just like the computer vision AI that classifies images as containing cars or other objects, ours will classify images that depict the vile abuse of children, so they can be flagged to police investigators. We do this not to attempt to replace or automate police with technology, but to add another tool to their arsenal for prosecuting what is a heinous, life-destroying crime. We are one of only a few teams worldwide that are engaged in this kind of research, and we have the advantage of a close partnership between law enforcement and academic research, so we can quickly validate our techniques in real-world situations. While this is a hugely difficult task, it's an absolute necessity to use technology to counter what is very much a technology-facilitated crime, one that unfortunately is growing almost exponentially.[21]

It's worth noting at the outset that most technological detection of child sexual abuse material (CSAM) is aimed at finding material *already known* to law enforcement. It's a disturbing fact that, due to the nature of the internet, CSAM is not just widely shared among offenders at the time of its creation, but it exists and continues to be shared for years afterwards. This is a form of perpetual re-abuse of victims. When these images and videos are seized by police, their digital signatures are stored and shared with law enforcement worldwide to enable their future rapid identification, in the event they reappear. As a safeguard, algorithms have been developed to generate the digital signatures in such a way that if these images are modified, as long as enough of their core content remains, they will still be flagged.[22]

At AiLECS, we are particularly interested in the identification of CSAM that has *never* been previously encountered by law enforcement. That is, we want a machine to learn to recognise such material using AI, as no digital signature will be available. On the face of it, the approach to this task, at least technically, mirrors the earlier description of how modern computer vision AI systems work: feed large quantities of the material to be analysed to the deep neural network algorithm during the training phase and have it learn to correctly classify it. And in our case, logically, this would appear to involve an AI ingesting masses of CSAM.

It seems flippant to say it, but dealing with such sensitive data is extremely difficult. In this case, the data graphically depicts the damage done to defenceless human beings. So, in our current stream of work, we have decided not to attempt to train AI systems directly on this data. Of course, we need the AI to be as accurate as it can be in flagging CSAM content. But while our law enforcement partners have tested the algorithms in real investigative scenarios, for all sorts of reasons we would like to see how far we can push the technology without it having 'seen' CSAM as such. After all, as human beings, we do not need to be directly exposed to such material in order to recognise it.

Instead, we decided to use what we consider 'proxy' data—that is, data that do not contain any illegal material itself—to identify CSAM. Simplifying things a bit, the premise is that if a computer can learn to detect sexual activity in general, such as through training on lawful adult sexual content, and if it can learn to detect the presence of children, via training on lawful images of children, we could then develop algorithms that flag as being of potential concern any images encountered where both of these things are present.

In constructing non-CSAM datasets that would be useful for training deep learning–based AI to recognise characteristics of CSAM, we first applied ourselves to the task of training and testing AI to detect the presence of a child or children in an image. This on its own is not a novel application of AI. Indeed, you are likely able to conduct a search of the photos on your phone based on the keyword 'child' using various proprietary AI algorithms. In our case, though, the child detection task is but one component of the overall detection pipeline, with our core research aimed at achieving higher accuracy for detecting CSAM specifically, and so we needed to build the system from the ground up. Almost immediately, an ethical dilemma presented itself.

We needed benign images of children, and we needed lots of them. Where was this data to come from? One obvious way to build a dataset of images of children is to download such images from the internet. This is exactly the approach taken in building large vision and language AI models. *Web scraping*, which is the use of software to automatically download internet content, usually at large scale, is a path well trodden by computer scientists in this domain. The underlying assumption is that, if the data are publicly accessible on the internet, then there shouldn't be a problem with using it. And anyway, where else could we source the large quantities of data needed for this task?

Well, it turns out there are lots of potential pitfalls with this approach.

The first problem we encountered was that of consent for the use of these images. Various legal issues seemed relevant, at least as far as they governed the public availability of the image in the first place. In particular, we were concerned that at least the consent of the child and a parent/guardian should be obtained if anything in the image is likely to be able to be used to identify the child. This could be a school uniform, or even the place where the image was taken.[23] Also, law enforcement agencies such as the AFP regularly caution against the online sharing of such images without proper access control.[24]

Web scraping to obtain data is typically very loosely constrained at best, a bit like trawler fishing. By scraping images, not only would we be unsure that appropriate consent for the initial posting of an image had been given, but we would have no mechanism for seeking consent for including it in a database for training AI that might be used by police for detecting illegal imagery. And, of course, as the internet is a global network, we would be downloading images from places where local laws on consent for publication of images of children online may differ from those in Australia. So although it may have proved to be the case that many of the images of children online do comply with various privacy regulations, and maybe the use of some of them would constitute a legal form of 'fair use', we were uncomfortable with proceeding.

It wasn't just the legal issues that troubled us. As we discussed how to undertake the data collection, concerns in many parts of the broader community around data use were clearly troubling the members of the lab too. Soon we were contemplating the idea that, beyond what was written in the relevant regulations, we needed to take a much more participatory approach to data collection, especially regarding our intended application of AI—one that was a world apart from scraping the web for images. When it came to images of children, it was clear that a far more ethical approach would be to explicitly ask for consent for the use of these images—not just to be compliant with privacy legislation, but to create an opportunity to inform those consenting about how their images were to be used. This would also give us the opportunity to thank them for contributing to the development of technology we hoped could make a difference in the fight against child exploitation.

We settled on a crowdsourcing mechanism we christened My Pictures Matter.[25] We called on adults to submit lawful, benign photos of themselves taken when they were children, asking them also to label the images with their age at the time of the photo. The idea was that these images would then form a key component of our training dataset to help our systems recognise the presence of children in unsafe situations. By asking adults to consent to the use of their own image (as a child), we sidestepped problematic considerations of having a child and/or parents and guardians agree to the use of the child's image.

Interestingly, the online comments on media coverage of My Pictures Matter have reflected quite a diversity of views.[26] Many see it as a laudable initiative that empowers people to contribute to the fight against child exploitation, some are concerned about police involvement in the project (although none of the data are stored on police systems), and others view the project as cringingly utopian or just impractical. The argument about the program being unworkable is understandable. After all, from a computer science standpoint, the pragmatic truth is that it's unrealistic to expect consent-driven, crowdsourced data collection to generate the same volume of training data as would be obtained by trawling the public web. In addition, many researchers and developers are keen to show that their models outperform all the others. However, with significant community engagement, we hope to curate a more limited dataset that will boost the performance of CSAM detection algorithms.

UNDER SURVEILLANCE

The importance of consensual engagement with AI can be magnified depending on the nature of the use of the AI. Some applications of AI are inherently more controversial than others. For example, it's important to note that with My Pictures Matter, we are in no way seeking to identify particular children. Having an AI detect whether or not any children may be present in an image is quite a different proposition to facial recognition that would pinpoint a child's identity. Facial recognition, particularly what is known as *one-to-many* facial recognition, whereby someone's identity is automatically inferred by matching it against a large database of faces, is a particularly fraught application of AI. Used to effect what is essentially biometric surveillance, it is the kind of AI application that has a lot of people worried. It is certainly more contentious than *one-to-one* facial recognition, whereby a face is analysed for a match against one identity only—this is the kind of facial recognition involved in logging into your phone, or being scanned at automatic passport control gates. Complicating matters is the fact that, at the time of writing, Australia does not have specific laws regulating the use of facial recognition, beyond provisions of the *Privacy Act*.[27]

It's not just governmental or law enforcement use of this technology—where it can be argued there is ostensibly more oversight—that has caused concern. Australian consumer advocacy group Choice raised eyebrows with a report in 2022 that exposed the use of facial recognition in retail chains

Kmart, Bunnings and The Good Guys.[28] The report found that most customers had no idea they were being surveilled—few saw or remembered what was noted as manifestly inadequate physical signage at store entrances. Bunnings argued that its facial recognition was designed to recognise individuals who had previously been involved in 'incidents of concern'. Although this is broadly akin to the use of facial recognition in, for example, casinos to enforce bans on individuals, and security applications at other premises, the move into more general retail settings represents for many a disturbing creep of the technology.

Taking things up a notch, another prominent example of the use of facial recognition is represented by Clearview AI, described by one media outlet as the 'world's most controversial company'.[29] Clearview's technology unashamedly advocates one-to-many facial recognition at enormous scale, with the system rapidly matching an uploaded image against a database of tens of billions of images scraped from public data sources on the internet. The software is marketed largely to law enforcement agencies and has had spectacular success in identifying offenders and disrupting serious crime. But in late 2021, Clearview found itself at the centre of a worldwide storm around privacy. The Office of the Australian Information Commissioner found that the company breached Australian privacy laws, with the commissioner stating: 'The indiscriminate scraping of people's facial images, only a fraction of whom would ever be connected with law enforcement investigations, may adversely impact the personal freedoms of all Australians who perceive themselves to be under surveillance.'[30]

At the time of writing, this ruling was being appealed by Clearview, but for now, use of the company's database in Australia is essentially banned. In the United States, a lawsuit led by the American Civil Liberties Union has seen Clearview agree to restrict the distribution of its database to local law enforcement agencies (while still marketing it to federal agencies). The sources of much of Clearview's data, Google and Facebook, have determined that the company breached the relevant terms of use and have demanded it cease scraping their sites for facial images. The debate around Clearview remains interesting, however, in that a clear public interest is being served by the apprehension of serious criminal offenders through use of the software, in addition to demonstrable benefits to community safety. The technology has been used in the pursuit of child abusers, and multiple children have been rescued from harm.

When there is such evidence that technology is saving lives, the question is how to effectively regulate it worldwide so that it can be used for these purposes, while at the same time upholding the human rights and privacy of individuals. Human rights should always be a consideration with respect to any technology. It's just that AI, and especially the pace of its development, is challenging regulators as they've never been challenged before.

Whether it is with respect to hot-button issues such as facial recognition or the other AI systems we interact with, the issue of consent is complicated. How many of us read the privacy policies associated with the myriad devices and apps that collect our personal information? It is also becoming increasingly difficult—or at least extremely inconvenient—to opt out of the AI-powered services we interact with. More and more of these services are being moved onto automated, algorithmic systems. Organisations known as *data brokers*, whose sole purpose is to buy and sell personal data, are part of a multibillion-dollar market that undoubtedly fuels much of AI.

Another consideration when it comes to all of this data harvesting is that the data need to be stored somewhere. Yet, more and more, dedicated data centres are being recognised as an environmental concern—they collectively contributed close to 1 per cent of global carbon dioxide emissions in 2021, a number that has likely risen since then.[31] Organisations also hold onto a lot of data they most likely don't need, sometimes in the pursuit of data-led AI decision-making that may have only a marginal impact on their operations. Historical data often do not get destroyed when they should, or data that are only needed for a one-time purpose are inappropriately retained. This produces numerous 'honeypots' of personal data around the world that are frequently breached, resulting in this data being leaked and used for nefarious purposes such as identity theft and other cybercrimes. Furthermore, almost every digital service asks users to create yet another account so their activities can be tracked and their data harvested—and likely fed into AI systems of various kinds for analyses and predictions. More data accounts means more personal data spread across the internet, and more opportunities for criminals to exploit this data.

Is it possible we have become the metaphorical slowly boiled frog with respect to the use of personal data by AI, perhaps only now beginning to realise that the temperature in our pot is uncomfortably high? And even if we have, do many of us really care how our data are being used? After all, by using Facebook, billions of people are freely sharing significant amounts of personal information, probably without much regard to how it is being used. Whether we *should* care is a personal issue, but it's hard to care about something if you don't know it's happening. And that's where we need a lot more transparency when it comes to how data, and the AI powered by it, are being used.

THE 'RESPONSIBLE AI' IMPERATIVE

You'd be right in thinking that some AI practitioners are worried about their public reputation as they increasingly seek to assure the public that they are involved solely in the development of 'responsible', 'trustworthy' or 'ethical' AI. While the ethical use of technology in general has a solid history of attracting interest from researchers, recently there has been a veritable explosion of fascination in the specific field of AI ethics. Reflecting this, in 2019 Australia adopted an AI Ethics Framework,[32] making us one of an increasing number of countries whose governments espouse such a framework. If we closely examine the issues that can cause AI to 'go wrong', it's understandable that such ethical guidelines have emerged so strongly in response to the national and global conversation around the potential dangers of AI.

'Garbage in, garbage out' is an overused but very apt phrase in data processing that indicates the complete dependency of computer programs on the quality of their input data. That is, it should not be expected that 'good' output from a program will result from 'bad' input to a program. However, depending on the area of application, the 'garbage out' of badly trained AI may not be simply nonsensical but could be manifestly harmful. Further, it's sometimes much harder to predict AI behaviour in all circumstances than it was for earlier generations of algorithms. AI systems, particularly if they have been hyped as a well-engineered technical solution to a complex problem, also can become the subject of a degree of blind faith among their users. So it may not be readily accepted by those same users that 'bad' outcomes are not just an artefact of the algorithm knowing best but rather are mostly a result of bad data.

What is sometimes termed *algorithmic bias*, or the unfairness of an algorithm in relation to particular individuals or groups, has concerned data scientists for many years. There have been well-publicised situations whereby the outputs of AI systems have been shown to exhibit various degrees of undesirable discrimination. In a purely computational sense, this can be the result of training data that is not a good statistical representation of the population. To work well, AI needs to be trained on data that best represents the environment it is working in. But the problem may be more than just a technical one. It's often the case that human biases in the building of training datasets mean the AI is essentially ingesting those world views, perhaps compromising objectivity.

When it comes to machine learning–based AI, if it is trained on poorly curated training data, such human biases may be magnified. This is true even if particular indicators such as race or gender, on which we certainly would want to avoid discrimination, are not explicitly recorded in the training data. Due to model complexity and human and technical factors in the training pipeline, it is also possible that an AI system could begin to discriminate in ways that its designers could not have anticipated, even with careful data curation. This behaviour may not be easily observed until the AI system has been in use for some time. Even simple algorithmic tools that would be categorised at the lower end of 'intelligence' or complexity are dangerous if they are relied on without proper oversight and consideration of the data they are ingesting.

A textbook example of a potentially biased AI system is the proprietary algorithmic tool known as Correctional Offender Management Profiling for Alternative Sanctions (COMPAS), which attracted significant media attention in 2016. COMPAS was (and still is) marketed to US courts as a tool that could predict the likelihood that a person appearing for sentencing would reoffend in the future. The tool held some promise. The estimation of such risk in a judge's mind is key to the decision-making process concerning the nature and duration of a criminal sentence. And there is a good argument to be made that a data-driven, decision-support system devoid of human fallibilities, biases and inconsistencies could provide a valuable input into the overall estimation of recidivism risk. COMPAS, however, generated controversy when a well-publicised independent analysis revealed that use of the algorithm exposed, rather than avoided, particular biases.[33] The headline result of this investigation was that black defendants were much more likely to be incorrectly classified by COMPAS as presenting a higher risk of reoffending than white defendants. The company behind COMPAS argued against this analysis, but given the closed-source nature of the tool, researchers could only examine its outputs, not its internal workings, and those outputs were of concern.

The COMPAS system is at least an advisory tool, rather than an autonomous sentencing judge. Situations where decisions are taken entirely by algorithms are potentially much more dangerous. The software engineering industry has long concerned itself with quality control in critical autonomous systems. If the software is to actually take the place of humans in the decision loop, then careful testing and oversight mechanisms are vital. Because of this, overall we are in a much better position because of autonomous systems designed to improve safety in many domains. For example, air travel has become safer and safer over many years with the increasing computerisation of the associated functions. But this is a high-stakes game—when things go wrong, they can do so in a terrible way, as commercial aircraft accidents due to deficiencies in automated systems inevitably remind us.

Closer to home, a massively disastrous implementation of completely automated decision-making—what some have described as an 'AI' failure—was the robodebt scheme run by Australia's social security agency, Centrelink. This scheme, which in August 2022 became the subject of a royal commission, wrongly alleged debts against individuals using an algorithm that inferred money might be owed to the Commonwealth based on a comparison of data from the Australian Taxation Office with Centrelink data. With little manual oversight, these debt notices were issued as a result of the software's 'decisions'. In 2021, the Australian Federal Court was told that well over A\$1.7 billion dollars in debt notices had been illegally raised against hundreds of thousands of individuals, and it approved this amount plus interest as part of a settlement package for those impacted.

The seriously detrimental effects, both financial and personal, of the robodebt scheme have been well documented. This was not a failure of an algorithm as such, however, but rather of deliberate human decision-making in the engineering and implementation of an automated system. Neither was the scheme's failure due to the difficulty of explaining a complex AI system whose internal workings are overly opaque (a so-called 'black box' system). In this case, the algorithms constructed were rudimentary and ignored many factors that could have more accurately estimated debt.[34]

While robodebt was a systemic failure of human oversight of an algorithmic deployment, other, more complex AI systems can fail in different ways. For all their recent successes, those AI-based chatbots I've discussed can easily go awry. They can generate completely incorrect assertions, blithely constructing them using confident-sounding language. In some cases they have spouted offensive statements, made threats, or generally appeared to not know what they are talking about. In fact, despite appearances, not only do they not know what they are talking about, it has been argued that they *can't* 'know' what they are talking about—not if the concept of knowledge implies understanding.

Take the 'intelligence' of large language models. Their output is based on statistical analyses via machine learning of large scrapes of text from the internet. In essence, this approach sees them predicting the 'best' next word over and over again to build up text. This is not exactly how human beings learn how to speak, nor is it how our intelligence works with respect to language. Some argue that large language models are internally constructing a representation of the world that is analogous to biological representations, but the jury is well and truly out on this. What is true is that, given these models are ingesting human-written text from the internet, it's unsurprising that they can produce text that isn't always useful, and that there's also a natural over-representation of those topics discussed more in the training dataset. Of more concern is the fact that, given the internet is hardly devoid of what could politely be called misinformation, any AI model trained on large swathes of it without careful curation, and training of the model for safety, may learn this misinformation and consequently cannot be relied on. Again, garbage in, garbage out—writ large.

TRANSLATING IDEALS INTO PRACTICE

There are plenty of AI failures that are not as dramatic or as visible as those I have already mentioned. As AI is scaled up and new models are developed, there is certainly much greater awareness of the potential societal impacts of AI and some of its modes of failure. Responsible AI initiatives in companies and research organisations, plus associated ethics statements, have grown out of consideration of the ramifications of AI failures and efforts to mitigate these. Australia's AI Ethics Framework outlines aspirational voluntary guidelines that should underpin the development and use of AI. These principles state, in summary, that AI should be: of benefit to humanity and the environment; respectful of human rights; fair; protective of people's privacy; safe and reliable; transparent and explainable; contestable; and accountable. Few would argue against these ideals. The tricky part is translating them into practical realities. The Australian Government freely acknowledges this, having observed business encounter complex challenges when trying to apply the pilot version of the AI ethics principles. It was (rather predictably) discovered that some of the principles were highly subjective and therefore difficult to put into action.

Of course, it's not just Australia that is grappling with the ethics of AI. The principles detailed in our own framework very much reflect those in other countries. However, given these guidelines tend to be so broad in their descriptions, mapping them not just to different industries and AI applications but also to different cultural contexts, is perilous. Large AI systems are often implemented across international boundaries or significantly varied societal norms. What's seen as 'ethical AI' (or at least subject to a perception of wide acceptance) in one place may well be seen quite differently elsewhere.

Furthermore, it has been pointed out that discussion around AI ethics needs to incorporate a greater degree of cultural diversity, because most of the current initiatives are peculiarly Western.[35] It's also not clear that there has been enough involvement of trained ethicists in the approaches being advocated. More broadly, there is a responsibility on AI researchers and developers to invite public debate on these issues, rather than hoping their own in-house guidelines meet community expectations. Any organisation wishing to deploy already developed AI systems that affect individuals or communities in any way, surely has a similar responsibility.

It's not the case that current AI ethics frameworks are worthless. They are certainly useful tools for framing thinking. But ultimately, as AI evolves and has an even greater impact, there will be a legitimate call for real regulation of its use beyond these optional 'guidelines for good'— AI-powered weapons are but the most obvious target for regulation. It's hard to know how many of the failures of AI in practice would not have happened if developers had run through a checklist of ethical principles. It seems unlikely that, in large organisations, questions of fairness, human oversight and transparency are steadfastly not considered. Still, building ethics into organisational systems, ways of working and accountability mechanisms remains vitally important. All of us should be encouraged to engage in the debate about the governance of AI.

Acting responsibly in the implementation of AI does not just mean the ethical deployment of systems and consideration of those affected by the *output* of AI. It's also possible for the process of AI development to cause harm *before* the system itself is put into practice. I've already spoken of issues of algorithmic bias and the misrepresentation of people through the collection of potentially skewed training data without their active involvement. But the training phase of AI can be even more hazardous. I alluded earlier to the fact that training data needs to be labelled; that is, the training phase for a machine learning algorithm requires a ground truth that sees a 'correct' label allocated to each data item in the training set. Then the algorithm can be trained so that it can eventually do its own labelling on previously unseen data and be correct in most cases. Often, these labels can be automatically harvested from a training database (or the internet) based on existing text, captions on images and audio, or inferred in some other way. But there is plenty of data out there, data on which developers want to train AI, that do not have explicit labels, nor can they be easily obtained. Someone has to do this labelling, and it is a mammoth task—so much so that an economy of sorts has grown up around data labelling, perhaps the best known example being Amazon's Mechanical Turk crowdsourcing labour service.[36]

Sometimes, though, what needs to be labelled is really nasty stuff. For example, in the quest to make AI safer, developers seek to have it learn what is unsafe. Someone therefore has to look at this unsafe material and label it as such. Remember also that AI needs a lot of data, which means human beings may need to look at large volumes of harmful material in order to help train the system to recognise it. Who's going to do this and how will it affect them? The answers here can be disturbing.

For example, in January 2023, *TIME* published an article documenting how OpenAI, the creators of ChatGPT, employed an outsourcing firm operating in Kenya to label internet-sourced text that it wanted its AI to find offensive and unsuitable for inclusion in output.[37] This included text that described in detail violent and abusive crimes, including the sexual abuse of children and instances of bestiality, and also suicide. The relationship between the outsourcing firm and OpenAI was eventually terminated, but not before workers were engaged for under US$2 per hour to review this material. It's hardly unusual for work to be globally outsourced in order to reduce costs. Doing so with respect to tasks known to have psychologically harmful effects requires that relevant mental health support mechanisms for workers are in place. But the *TIME* article indicated that some Kenyan workers told journalists that some of the help offered was manifestly inadequate.

WEAPONISING AI

Beyond those cases of AI having unintended deleterious effects, and as is the case with all tools, AI can be deliberately used to cause harm. One way of literally weaponising AI is exhibited by its use in the algorithmic control of lethal armaments. The biggest concern here is not just the use of AI in systems that augment existing human-controlled military systems, but that of fully autonomous AI-powered weapons. Those same machine learning algorithms that are so adept at real-world object recognition for, say, autonomous vehicles can just as easily be repurposed so that instead of having a car avoid a pedestrian, a weapon is fired at a person or a group of people.

If you want to be terrified about the possible future trajectory of autonomous AI weapons, seek out the short film *Slaughterbots* online. This production by the not-for-profit Future of Life Institute generated significant interest (and alarm) when it was released in 2017. The film (as with its 2021 follow-up) presents fictional scenarios of AI-powered drones making and carrying out decisions as to who they should kill, but this future is potentially a lot closer than you might think.

A number of reports have surfaced describing the use of AI weapons in real conflicts. In 2021, the United Nations Security Council reported that an AI-guided military drone was believed to have been used to attack military targets in Libya without 'requiring data connectivity between the operator and the munition: in effect, a true "fire, forget and find" capability'.[38] The full autonomy of these weapons means that it is entirely up to an AI algorithm to decide on the targets—no human needs to be involved beyond the initial launch of the weapon into the sphere of combat. In the case of autonomous drone weapons, they also can be used to form communicating swarms, thus magnifying their algorithmically governed destructive power. Some of the makers of these weapons platforms have been open with respect to their capacity not just to inflict damage on general military targets, but how inbuilt facial recognition enables them to precisely target individuals as well.

The handing over to a machine of responsibility for decisions about who to kill poses a massive ethical and regulatory challenge to governments. Although it can be argued that such weaponry can be more precise and less indiscriminate than human-fired weapons, nonetheless there have been widespread calls to ban them outright due to the lack of human agency in their use. The International Committee of the Red Cross called for a prohibition on what it described as 'unpredictable' autonomous weapons, including those that use machine learning to identify new targets.[39] Efforts to establish an international treaty governing the use of such arms are ongoing, with seventy nations delivering a joint statement to the United Nations in 2022 requesting that all member states 'intensify consideration' of the issue of lethal autonomous weapons.[40] Needless to say, beyond any future, lawfully governed proliferation of such weapons, their potential use by criminals and terrorists poses very serious threats to society.

Lethal autonomous weapons sit at the extreme end of a broad spectrum describing the possible malicious uses of AI. Elsewhere on this spectrum is the application of AI in generating misinformation. One particularly harmful form of this is represented by the advent of faked media using deep learning–based AI—so-called *deepfakes*. This technology, which is becoming more and more powerful, is capable of producing highly realistic images and videos. One way in which deepfakes can be created is through the use of an algorithm known as *generative adversarial networks*. Two neural network algorithms essentially fight with each other to get better at their tasks, with one of them generating a faked image and the other trying to detect the fake. As the detector gets better at identifying the fake, the faker gets better at learning how to fool the detector, and through this kind of algorithmic arms race, a highly realistic deepfake is produced.

Accompanying the early study of deepfake generation were algorithms that could detect them. In 2020 came the launch of the Deepfake Detection Challenge, governed by the not-for-profit Partnership for AI.[41] A large dataset of deepfakes was created by Facebook (Meta) and made available to the worldwide research community. Vying for US$1 million in total prize money, researchers were tasked with developing their own algorithms for detecting which videos were fake and which were real. As well as the submitted algorithms being trained and tested using the public dataset, they were also evaluated for rigour on what was described as a black box dataset, which contained deepfakes that had never been seen by the competitors. The challenge generated enormous interest, with well over 8000 entries. But the results emphasised that detecting deepfakes is not easy—the winning algorithm was able to correctly detect only 65 per cent of the deepfakes in the black box dataset.

Since 2020, deepfake-detection algorithms have improved. In 2022, Intel claimed its FakeCatcher technology was 96 per cent accurate in detecting deepfakes in real time.[42] (Some, though, have seriously questioned its efficacy in real-world scenarios.[43]) This kind of tool could be very valuable for deployment in, say, news organisations or video-distribution platforms. However, as detection algorithms improve, so do deepfake generation algorithms. In the rapidly developing area of misinformation, one thing is clear: even if detection algorithms get to the point where they are uniformly reliable and trusted, they would need to be deployed *everywhere* to fight the distribution of deepfakes. It is disturbingly likely that we are not far away from the point where our human eyes are just not going to be enough to distinguish between what's real and what's not in venues we previously would have trusted implicitly.

There are concerns about deepfaked material being used for political purposes, undermining societal stability through, for example, the creation of believable yet fictional communications from government leaders. However, according to one widely publicised report, by far the most prevalent form of deepfake today is AI-generated pornography.[44] This has powered a rise in technology-facilitated abuse involving the non-consensual making and sharing of realistic-looking but fake pornographic images of real people. Many countries are scrambling to outlaw this hugely damaging activity—including Australia, with its recently updated online safety legislation.[45]

If that doesn't sound bad enough, a further disturbing possibility of deepfake technology is the creation of fake child sexual abuse material. Virtual or animated CSAM is already illegal in many jurisdictions—it certainly is in Australia. The hyperrealism of the image generation technology used to create deepfakes may take this crime to a new level, including the targeting of actual children so they are realistically portrayed in sexualised and abusive situations. Just like animated CSAM, even if the abusive acts themselves did not take place, this material perpetuates and amplifies such abuse, and dehumanises victims. That's pretty scary stuff.

AI AS ARTIST?

Let's take a deep breath. The vast majority of AI developers don't want to do us harm (at least, not deliberately). Indeed, some of them seek to inspire us and are exploring how the technology can produce what we mere humans call art. Long before AI became so powerful, computer software provided artists with tools that opened up creative possibilities. From the programming of a US air-defence computer via punch cards in 1956 to render a cathode-ray version of an *Esquire* magazine model,[46] through the proliferation of computer-generated imagery in film and television, and all manner of artistic experiments along the way, the world is no stranger to the use of computers in the visual arts.

But with modern AI, computers can be much more than the providers of tools to enhance the work of artists. They can facilitate the generation of never-before-seen images with very little input, because we are now in the era of autonomous art derived through generative AI. Of course, an AI artist is not exactly a computerised facsimile of a painter pouring emotion onto a canvas, seeking to capture the aching longings of the robot condition. Far from it. Generative AI is palpably more derivative than the work of humans who channel artistic inspiration from others. It is a mimic on a grand scale, and once it's trained on (you guessed it) enormous amounts of data, it doesn't need much input to get started. Using one of the recently developed and highly ingenious generative machine learning models, AI can literally learn how to paint a picture with words: no paintbrush, camera or artistic talent required. These models take only natural language prompts as input—think 'painting of a sailing boat' or 'painting of a sailing boat in the style of Picasso' or even 'a realistic image of a mouse driving a taxi'. The AI will then get to work and quickly produce some startling results. Much more benign in intent compared with the novel image construction of deepfakes, these artistic AI image generators—including Stable Diffusion, DALL-E 2, Midjourney, Imagen and the popular phone app Lensa—have taken the internet by storm along with their text-generating cousins in recent years.

Now, what of the enormous amount of data they learn from? As is usually the case, these AI systems are voraciously hungry during training, needing upwards of hundreds of millions of images and associated text labels. This means that via web scraping, they are ingesting images that have been created in a myriad ways. If AI is going to create art that we can appreciate, it needs to be fed with art that we already appreciate. But did all of those AI developers ask for artists to actively contribute their works for this purpose? No. That would take too long and there probably wouldn't be enough data. So with the rise of generative AI, infringing as it does on the domain of human artists, legal and moral issues of consent for the use of data have rapidly become apparent. In particular, a dataset with the enigmatic name LAION-5B, containing links to well over five billion publicly accessible internet images for use in training AI, quickly came under fire from the artistic community. This database is not the only such source of training data, but it's one of the biggest and is easily available to everyone online. Many artists have argued in essence that the inclusion of their original works in this massive collection, and its subsequent use for generative AI, mean they are being ripped off and their copyright infringed upon. This is most acutely the case with respect to AI systems that generate paintings which intentionally simulate the style of an existing artist. The law is yet to catch up to all this,[47] although in January 2023, three artists launched litigation against some of the makers of these tools.[48]

The argument made by creators that this indiscriminate web scraping of artworks for AI training is at the very least unethical, seems compelling. After all, often the developers of these systems are rapidly generating income off the back of human-created artwork. In response, the website Have I Been Trained? has been set up as a front-end through which artists (and anyone else) can search for images in the LAION-5B database. This has already led to the discovery of not just plenty of linked copyrighted material but even private medical photos.[49] The presence of such images as links in the training database is arguably not the responsibility of the database administrators, as they do not host the material directly. But how does this argument sit with the fact that deliberate and automatic web scraping at scale was undertaken, such that problematic issues like this were difficult to detect, and that links to such images were provided without further significant restriction in a single database for training AI?

Music is not escaping the clutches of generative AI either. A potential gift to those of us with no musical ability, Google is leading the way with MusicLM,[50] which is capable of generating music clips purely from text descriptions. The source data used to train this model came from 280 000 hours of human-generated music and associated text descriptions. Interestingly, in this case, an ethical (and legal) handbrake is being applied. Google has stated it is concerned about the impact of this technology on the music industry, including possible cultural appropriation and copyright infringement. So, as of January 2023, it was only releasing small samples of the output of MusicLM publicly, not the full AI model. (My favourite sample is that generated from the test input 'accordion death metal'.)

The music production landscape is awash, however, with all sorts of AI tools that don't set out to generate an entire composition simply from text like MusicLM. Rather, these tools use machine learning to enhance or otherwise manipulate existing elements of a song. Relatively inexpensive AI-based software trained on the desired characteristics of particular types of music is starting to do a reasonable job of automating many tasks of producers and sound engineers. Increasingly, algorithmic manipulation of singing voices is a feature of popular music—computer-based pitch correction is almost universally employed to some extent in commercial songs. Although these algorithms could barely be described as AI themselves, an AI tool was recently developed to detect when they have been used.[51] At least AI can tell us how our music has been processed, even if it didn't write it.

THE QUESTION OF EXPLAINABILITY

When we interact with AI, we are surely entitled to expect accountability and transparency, just as we would from human interactions. Autonomous algorithmic decision-making presents challenges in this regard and so needs to be carefully governed. A key concern that impacts the transparency of deep learning AI models is that they are so manifestly complex. Remember, these are highly connected neural networks with billions of parameters tuned through many training iterations. Even very simple neural networks are very sophisticated function approximators—deep learning takes this complexity up several notches.

A common refrain, then, is that the output of these systems cannot be easily *explained*. Specifically, it can be very difficult to clarify how the algorithm came to its decision, why it classified a particular input in a particular way, or how a given set of data contributed to its overall learning—in other words, how the algorithm did its 'reasoning'. This is not to say we don't understand the architecture of the network or the procedures that govern the updating of parameters—after all, these were designed and coded by humans. But, in the example context of deep learning, once data—let's say images—are given to the network in a training phase, we are limited in our ability to explain how they are dealt with. The best we can do is some variant of 'The pixels in the image were processed in such a way that the network adjusted its parameters to minimise the difference between the ultimate classification of the image and its desired classification'. This may be sufficient for some situations, but for others—such as when an algorithm needs to be relied on in court—it will not provide anywhere near the desired level of understanding. The problem is that there's not a lot more that can be said about the algorithm itself. Ultimately, we are dealing with a situation akin to asking how a human being recognised another person in a police line-up. Our 'explanation' would be that we believe we have witnessed the person in some context of interest to the police. In this case, our biological neural networks have encoded this in some way, the internal mechanism of which it is not necessary for us to explain (or understand) in detail.

Of course, AI is not biological but rather is a deliberate, human-designed and human-engineered construct. And if it's replacing people in a decision loop, then understanding as much as possible how it arrived at its output is extremely important. A large, and growing, body of research on 'explainable AI' is attempting to address this problem. Consequently, a number of emerging techniques can be employed to make AI results more easily interpretable. But some aspects, like the fundamental difficulty in unpacking the inner workings of deep neural networks, will always remain an artefact of the algorithm's architecture.

A trade-off that can be made lies between how easy an AI model is to explain and its internal complexity; that is, less complex models are (usually) easier to interpret. Even small neural network models are relatively intricate, but there are other types of models we could deploy for particular purposes. For example, a 'decision tree' AI model forms a kind of visual map of how decisions are reached by an algorithm, and that visualisation can itself provide us with a handy explanation of how the AI is working. Unfortunately, when making predictions based on unstructured datasets, decision trees don't tend to work as well as deep neural networks. The trade-off, then, is not always only explainability versus the complexity of a model, but sometimes explainability versus the efficacy of a model. There are also other classes of

AI models that encode within their structure the relationship between events in the world in terms of estimated probabilities, and which can then be used to make predictions. These are powerful as well as relatively transparent and explainable AI models. But while they can be automatically constructed, depending on the application, they often require a large amount of human input in terms of tuning to ensure they are best representing the real-world event probabilities. And therein lies yet another trade-off, between explainability and the resources required to actually deploy the AI model in practice.

Understanding what is really going on in an AI system as a whole is vital if we are to trust it. But the AI 'system' is not *just* the algorithm. Fortunately, depending on the purpose of the AI system, explaining how that possibly very opaque algorithm is working is often not the only thing that is important. It turns out there's a lot more that can be done to provide valuable explanations and transparent reporting on the use of AI. AI systems always exist in a broader context, as part of a pipeline of sorts that includes the sourcing and construction of the training data. It can be the explanation of how this pipeline works that is crucial to documenting the AI in practice. This could include analysing the input data and visualising how different types or classes of data are distributed in the training dataset. This is important in exposing as much as possible any bias in the data: where did the data come from, how was it curated and was consent sought for its use? The labelling process also needs to be well documented: how was diversity in the labelling workforce ensured, and how were any discrepancies in labelling judgement dealt with? These and many other questions can and must be answered to ensure overall transparency of the AI training pipeline. In addition, beyond training the system, how is the use of the AI governed once it has been trained? How do people contest its decisions? How is it retrained when necessary? Explainability and transparency have many dimensions and beg just as many questions.

And, beyond all of these considerations, there are certain situations where the explanation that *really* needs to be made is this: just because we can use AI, should we?

LIVING WITH AI

There are plenty of diverse examples of AI in use today, with many more emerging all the time. We will undoubtedly interact more often with AI in the future. The technology will continue to provide powerful, useful tools across many domains. And for the most part, these tools will be broadly beneficial. However, this assertion presupposes that the risks of AI misuse will have been carefully considered and mitigated. This objective must not be assumed but rather actively pursued. It is also incumbent on those researching and developing these technologies to participate in the public conversation about AI in a way that explains and appropriately contextualises them. All communities need to talk more about AI, especially when autonomous decision-making that affects them is involved. This discussion needs leadership, but its stewards cannot be those who simply have a vested financial interest in pushing ahead with AI development—there needs to be as much focus on AI's costs as on its benefits.

While there's plenty of technological determinism at play in discussions around AI, there's also some pretty wild scaremongering. The vast middle ground is where the Australian and international discussions of AI need to take place. Here, governments have a clear role to play, in particular with respect to the appropriate regulation of harmful AI applications. The challenge is that the pace of development (and updating) of the appropriate regulatory regimes is likely to be outstripped by the pace of development of AI itself.

It's not possible to divorce the concept of living with AI from the concept of living within a 'datafied' society. As I've discussed, many AI systems are powerful because they are ingesting and learning from reams of data we have ourselves generated. The abilities of the massively connected deep neural networks that are the engine of so much modern AI are a result of not just their structure but also the quality of what they are fed as input. And for some of the purposes they are designed for, it's because of another massively connected structure—the internet—that those demands for data are met. This means that all of us whose data is available on the open internet, in social media or hosted in databases, and used in any way for training AI, are more than just observant bystanders in the development of this technology—we are actual participants. AI is built in many cases for significant monetary gain by its developers. It also may be used in ways that are incongruent with our personal values. We are therefore entitled to understand how our data are being used for training and testing AI, and for what purpose that AI is to be deployed.

Does living with AI mean reduced human agency and influence over decision-making? Does it mean surrendering our personal data in the process? Does it mean accepting opaque, poorly explained algorithms and systems? It might, but only to the extent we want it to. It might sound obvious, but we have a choice when it comes to the destiny of AI in our lives. This begins with not falling for anthropomorphic tropes that make out AI as some sort of 'other' beyond us. Ultimately, all AI successes are human successes and all AI failures are human failures. We need to deepen our discussion of AI, empower those it affects, advocate for fairness in its use, and along the way, let's not forget to take plenty of reality checks.

ACKNOWLEDGEMENTS

I'd like to thank Greg Bain for asking me to write this book in the first place, and Paul Smitz for his masterful editing. To all my colleagues in the AiLECS Lab, in particular Janis Dalins, thank you for our many conversations on how AI can make a positive difference in the face of serious societal threats. To Jennifer, thank you for your unwavering support.

NOTES

1   ChatGPT, 2023, https://chat.openai.com (viewed March 2023).

2   Stanford Institute for Human Centered Artificial Intelligence, *Artificial Intelligence Index Report 2022*, 2022, https://aiindex.stanford.edu/wp-content/uploads/2022/03/2022-AI-Index-Report_Master.pdf (viewed March 2023).

3   McKinsey, *The State of AI in 2022: and a Half Decade in Review*, 2022, https://www.mckinsey.com/capabilities/quantumblack/our-insights/the-state-of-ai-in-2022-and-a-half-decade-in-review (viewed March 2023).

4   PwC, *Sizing the Prize: What's the Real Value of AI for Your Business and How Can You Capitalise?*, 2017, https://www.pwc.com/gx/en/issues/data-and-analytics/publications/artificial-intelligence-study.html (viewed March 2023).

5   The idea of the digital computer wasn't even that new in the mid twentieth century. The English engineer Charles Babbage formulated the design for his Analytical Engine a century earlier. But the realisation of the first programmable digital computer had to wait until the

development of viable electronic mechanisms to represent, store and process digital data.

6   Alan Turing, 'Computing Machinery and Intelligence', *Mind*, vol. 59, no. 236, October 1950, pp. 433–60.

7   I make use of the term 'system' to indicate that implementation of AI is typically in the context of an information technology environment that includes various components for data collection, data management, computation and visualisation of results, in addition to the implementation of the AI algorithm(s).

8   By the way, AI doesn't just help you find photos. It's involved when you take them as well: see Kyle Chayka, 'Have iPhone Cameras Become too Smart?', *The New Yorker*, 18 March 2022, https://www.newyorker.com/culture/infinite-scroll/have-iphone-cameras-become-too-smart (viewed March 2023).

9   Alex Hern, 'Stephen Hawking: AI Will Be "Either Best or Worst Thing" for Humanity', *The Guardian Australia*, 20 October 2016, https://www.theguardian.com/science/2016/oct/19/stephen-hawking-ai-best-or-worst-thing-for-humanity-cambridge (viewed March 2023).

10 Sam Shead, 'Elon Musk Says Production of Tesla's Robot Could Start Next Year, But AI Experts Have Their Doubts', *CNBC*, 8 April 2022, https://www.cnbc.com/2022/04/08/elon-musk-says-tesla-is-aiming-to-start-production-on-optimus-next-year.html (viewed March 2023).

11 Nick Summers, 'Microsoft's Tay Is an AI Chat Bot with "Zero Chill"', *engadget*, 23 March 2016, https://www.engadget.com/2016-03-23-microsofts-tay-ai-chat-bot.html (viewed March 2023).

12 Andrew White, 'Our Top Data and Analytics Predicts for 2019', Gartner, 3 January 2019, https://blogs.gartner.com/andrew_white/2019/01/03/our-top-data-and-analytics-predicts-for-2019 (viewed March 2023).

13 Michael Atleson, 'Keep Your AI Claims in Check', Federal Trade Commission, 27 February 2023, https://www.ftc.gov/business-guidance/blog/2023/02/keep-your-ai-claims-check (viewed March 2023).

14 Sam Altman, 'Planning for AGI and Beyond', OpenAI, 24 February 2023, https://openai.com/blog/planning-for-agi-and-beyond (viewed March 2023).

15 It's worth noting, however, that more complex models don't always mean better performance.

16 Technically, 'tokens'—groups of characters that may be words or parts of words or other groups of characters in the text.

17 Wikipedia, 'Size of Wikipedia', 1 March 2023, https://en.wikipedia.org/wiki/Wikipedia:Size_of_Wikipedia (viewed March 2023).

18 Stable Diffusion Online, March 2023, https://stablediffusionweb.com (viewed March 2023).

19 Cisco, *Cisco Annual Internet Report (2018–2023) White Paper*, 9 March 2020, https://www.cisco.com/c/en/us/solutions/collateral/executive-perspectives/annual-internet-report/white-paper-c11-741490.html (viewed March 2023).

20 This is hard to estimate but see, for example, Internet Live Stats, 'Total Number of Websites', 15 March 2023, https://www.internetlivestats.com/total-number-of-websites (viewed March 2023).

21 International Centre for Missing and Exploited Children Australia, 'The Growing Global Threat of Child Sexual Abuse Material (CSAM)', 13 December 2021, https://icmec.org.au/blog/the-growing-global-threat-of-child-sexual-abuse-material-csam/ (viewed March 2023).

22 See, for example, Apple Inc., 'CSAM Detection: Technical Summary', August 2021, https://www.apple.com/child-safety/pdf/CSAM_Detection_Technical_Summary.pdf (viewed March 2023).

23 See for example https://aifs.gov.au/resources/resource-sheets/images-children-and-young-people-online

24 https://www.afp.gov.au/news-media/media-releases/afp-reminds-parents-think-posting-back-school-images-online

25 AiLECS Lab, 'My Pictures Matter', 2023, https://mypicturesmatter.org (viewed March 2023).

26 See Asha Barabaschow, 'The AFP Wants Pics of Younger You to Help Train Its Child Abuse-Thwarting Algorithm', *Gizmodo*, 3 June 2022, https://www.gizmodo.com.au/2022/06/my-pictures-matter-campaign (viewed March 2023); and Katyanna Quach, 'Police Lab Wants Your Happy Childhood Pictures to Train AI to Detect Child Abuse', *The Register*, 3 June 2022, https://www.theregister.com/2022/06/03/police_australia_ai (viewed March 2023).

27 That said, a model law has been proposed: see University of Technology Sydney, 'Facial Recognition Technology: Towards a Model Law', 27 September 2022, https://www.uts.edu.au/human-technology-institute/explore-our-work/facial-recognition-technology-towards-model-law (viewed March 2023).

28 Jarni Blakkarly, 'Kmart, Bunnings and The Good Guys Using Facial Recognition Technology in Stores', *Choice*, 12 July 2022, https://www.choice.com.au/consumers-and-data/data-collection-and-use/how-your-data-is-used/articles/kmart-bunnings-and-the-good-guys-using-facial-recognition-technology-in-store (viewed March 2023).

29 Jessica Mudditt, 'Meet the CEO of the World's Most Controversial Company, Clearview AI', *Forbes Australia*, 24 November 2022, https://www.forbes.com.au/covers/innovation/the-photos-that-speak-volumes (viewed March 2023).

30 Office of the Australian Information Commissioner, 'Clearview AI Breached Australians' Privacy', 3 November 2021, https://www.oaic.gov.au/updates/news-and-media/clearview-ai-breached-australians-privacy (viewed March 2023).

31 Asaf Ezra, 'Renewable Energy Alone Can't Address Data Centers' Adverse Environmental Impact', Forbes, 3 May 2021, https://www.forbes.com/sites/forbestechcouncil/2021/05/03/renewable-energy-alone-cant-address-data-centers-adverse-environmental-impact/?sh=523ca5e35ddc (viewed March 2023).

32 Australian Department of Industry, Science and Resources, 'Australia's Artificial Intelligence Ethics Framework', 7 November 2019, https://www.industry.gov.au/publications/australias-artificial-intelligence-ethics-framework (viewed March 2023).

33 Julia Angwin et al., 'Machine Bias', ProPublica, 23 May 2016, https://www.propublica.org/article/machine-bias-risk-assessments-in-criminal-sentencing (viewed March 2023).

34 Dr Tapani Rinta-Kahila et al., 'How to Avoid Algorithmic Decision-Making Mistakes: Lessons from the Robodebt Debacle', *Momentum* magazine, University of Queensland, n.d., https://stories.uq.edu.au/momentum-magazine/robodebt-algorithmic-decision-making-mistakes/index.html (viewed March 2023).

35 Emmanuel R Goffi, 'The Importance of Cultural Diversity in AI Ethics', *Beyond the Horizon*, 26 January 2021, https://behorizon.org/the-importance-of-cultural-diversity-in-ai-ethics (viewed March 2023).

36 Amazon Mechanical Turk, 2023, https://www.mturk.com (viewed March 2023).

37 Billy Perrigo, 'OpenAI Used Kenyan Workers on Less Than $2 Per Hour to Make ChatGPT Less Toxic', *TIME*,

18 January 2023, https://time.com/6247678/openai-chatgpt-kenya-workers (viewed March 2023).

38 United Nations Security Council, 'Letter Dated 8 March 2021 from the Panel of Experts on Libya', 8 March 2021, https://undocs.org/Home/Mobile?FinalSymbol=S%2F2021%2F229&Language=E&DeviceType=Desktop&LangRequested=False (viewed March 2023).

39 International Committee of the Red Cross, 26 July 2022, 'What You Need to Know about Autonomous Weapons', https://www.icrc.org/en/document/what-you-need-know-about-autonomous-weapons (viewed March 2023).

40 Emma Farge, 'UN Talks Adjourn without Deal to Regulate "Killer Robots"', 18 December 2021, https://www.reuters.com/article/us-un-disarmament-idAFKBN2IW1UJ (viewed March 2023).

41 Partnership on AI, 2023, https://partnershiponai.org (viewed March 2023).

42 Intel, 'Intel Introduces Real-Time Deepfake Detector', 14 November 2022, https://www.intel.com/content/www/us/en/newsroom/news/intel-introduces-real-time-deepfake-detector.html (viewed March 2023).

43 Esther Ajao, 'Intel Deepfake Detector Raises Questions', TechTarget, 14 November 2022, https://www.techtarget.com/searchenterpriseai/news/252527266/Intel-deepfake-detector-raises-questions (viewed March 2023).

44 Henry Ajder et al., *The State of Deepfakes: Landscapes, Threats and Impact*, Deeptrace, September 2019, https://regmedia.co.uk/2019/10/08/deepfake_report.pdf (viewed March 2023).

45 Alex Hern, 'Online Safety Bill Will Criminalise "Downblousing" and "Deepfake" Porn', *The Guardian*, 25 November 2022, https://www.theguardian.com/technology/2022/nov/24/online-safety-bill-to-return-to-parliament-next-month (viewed March 2023).

46 Benj Edwards, 'The Never-Before-Told Story of the
    World's First Computer Art (It's a Sexy Dame)', *The
    Atlantic*, 24 January 2013, https://www.theatlantic.com/
    technology/archive/2013/01/the-never-before-told-story-
    of-the-worlds-first-computer-art-its-a-sexy-dame/267439
    (viewed March 2023).

47 Barry Scannell, 'What Legal Implications Await Generative
    AI in 2023?', *Silicon Republic*, 14 February 2023, https://
    www.siliconrepublic.com/machines/william-fry-
    generative-ai-legal-trends-2023 (viewed March 2023).

48 James Vincent, 'AI Art Tools Stable Diffusion and
    Midjourney Targeted with Copyright Lawsuit', *The Verge*,
    16 January 2023, https://www.theverge.com/2023/1/
    16/23557098/generative-ai-art-copyright-legal-lawsuit-
    stable-diffusion-midjourney-deviantart (viewed March
    2023).

49 Benj Edwards, 'Artist Finds Private Medical Record
    Photos in Popular AI Training Data Set', *Ars Technica*,
    22 September 2022, https://arstechnica.com/information-
    technology/2022/09/artist-finds-private-medical-record-
    photos-in-popular-ai-training-data-set (viewed March
    2023).

50 Andrea Agostinelli et al., 'MusicLM: Generating Music
    from Text', Google Research, n.d., https://google-research.
    github.io/seanet/musiclm/examples (viewed March
    2023).

51 Will Betts, 'AI Can Now Detect Autotune: Here's What
    That Means', *Musiio Blog*, 12 May 2022, https://blog.
    musiio.com/2022/05/12/explaining-autotune-classifier
    (viewed March 2023).

IN THE NATIONAL INTEREST

Other books on the issues that matter: